Crafted *in* Faith

MONICA STOLTZFUS

Paige Tate & Co.

Copyright © 2025 Monica Stoltzfus
Published by Paige Tate & Co.
Paige Tate & Co. is an imprint of Blue Star Press
PO Box 8835, Bend, OR 97708
contact@paigetate.com
www.paigetate.com

Designed by Chancy Cannon
ISBN: 9781963183122

Printed in Colombia
10 9 8 7 6 5 4 3 2 1

The authorized representative in the EU for product safety and compliance
is Authorised Rep Compliance Ltd., Ground Floor, 71 Lower Baggot Street,
Dublin D02 P593, Ireland. www.arccompliance.com

"For we are God's handiwork,
created in Christ Jesus to
do good works, which God
prepared in advance
for us to do."

Ephesians 2:10
(New International Version)

Contents

"So, whether you eat or drink, or whatever you do, do all to the glory of God."

1 Corinthians 10:31

Introduction

I read this verse in my morning devotional after hearing the words "making time for God" in a dream. I believe the two are intrinsically connected. It doesn't matter whether we are working, eating, hanging out with friends, or doing any other type of activity—yes, even crafting—this verse speaks to how everything we do can be done for the glory of God. Everything!

For me, when my table is covered in glitter, glue, paper scraps, watercolor brushes, and much more, I feel alive. I feel like my heart is on fire with the gift of creativity that God has given me. And what are we called to do with our gifts? Let them shine and point to the One who created it all. So, I teach, share, and post to encourage those around me with the inspiration I've been given. I encourage others to work with their hands and now, by adding Bible verses, to work with their hearts. Each of these thirty crafts can deepen your relationship with our Maker through experiencing the creative process and trusting in the outcome. When the craft is complete, a connection has been made.

Happy making!

Hospitality

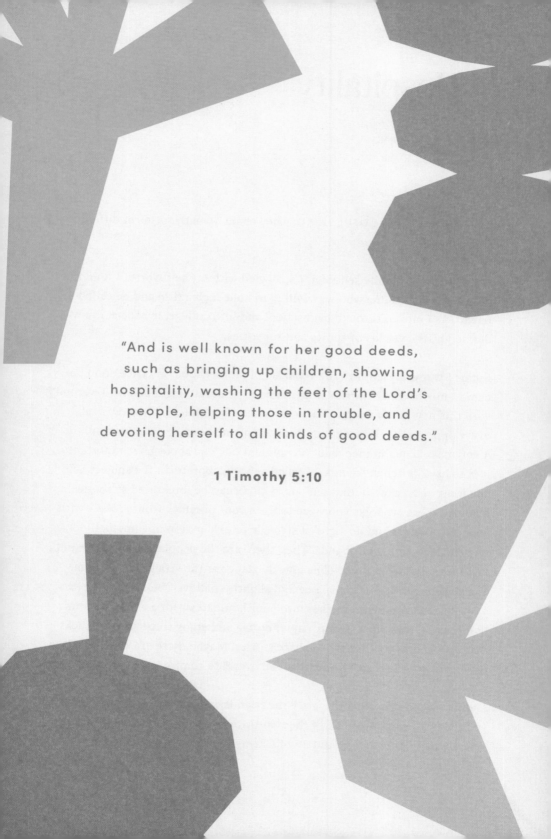

"And is well known for her good deeds, such as bringing up children, showing hospitality, washing the feet of the Lord's people, helping those in trouble, and devoting herself to all kinds of good deeds."

1 Timothy 5:10

➤ Hospitality

FRIENDS ARE A BEAUTIFUL THING. They come in many forms at different times in our lives.

As an awkward middle schooler, I struggled with my self-worth. I found it difficult to determine who was willing to hold such a title and be called my friend. As I moved through high school and into college, my social life was defined by the worlds of sports and sororities.

But as I threw myself into the vocation of motherhood, my tribe soon became a mix of other warrior women and my closest neighbors. All I wanted with this new set of friends was to welcome them into my home. So, at every opportunity, I opened my door to anyone needing a companion. A very dear acquaintance made a comment one day about how important it is to have "kitchen friends." I asked her to elaborate on the subject, and she went on to explain that our social circle can be illustrated as rooms in a home. There are folks you wave to from your porch or front stoop—with your hair perfect and no signs of struggle or exhaustion in your shoulders, on your face, or in your hands. Then there are the people you invite in, but just inside the front door. They quickly glance at the straightened rooms, and the conversations are sparse and slightly shallow. Then, there are just a few friends you invite further into your home to sit for a while. In your living room, they sip a steamy cup of coffee and enjoy some savory snacks on the couch as you listen and share stories. Maybe there are some children playing at your feet and toys strewn all over. It's comfortable.

And just when you think these are the friends who've seen it all and know you the best, you invite one of them into your kitchen. The dishes in the sink are dirty, there's a mountain of Cheerios on the floor, a calendar displaying the wrong month is hanging on the wall, a basket of overflowing laundry has become a child's seat at the table, and there are a few cobwebs in the crevices of the back window. This is where you live. This is real life. And you've invited someone to see it. This friend sees you in the midst of your battles, your unfinished projects, your dirty dishes, and your unmatched socks, and they love you more for it. These are the dear friends whom Jesus wants you to keep close.

But could there be more?

Is there someone you've waved to each morning from your porch steps who might have more to share if they were invited in? What would happen if you tried opening your home and your heart and welcomed, with whimsical hospitality, those who might be hurting or in need of healing or a hug?

_____

_____

_____

_____

_____

_____

_____

_____

_____

_____

_____

_____

_____

_____

_____

_____

_____

_____

_____

_____

Craft: Stamped Tea Towels

MATERIALS

A fresh lime or other citrus fruit
Cotton tea towel
Acrylic paint
Craft paintbrush
Fabric Mod Podge
Cutting board and knife
Iron

INSTRUCTIONS

1. Cut the lime or other citrus fruit in half.

2. Carve out the meaty part of the fruit, leaving the triangle membranes intact.

3. Squeeze out the extra juice and then dab the fruit on a paper towel to dry.

4. Mix one part Fabric Mod Podge with two parts acrylic paint. Stir well.

5. Use your paintbrush to paint the mix onto the lime half and all its triangle parts.

6. Immediately press the lime half down on the tea towel in a few spaced-out areas or your desired pattern.

7. Let the tea towel dry for twenty-four hours. Then, place another towel on top of your tea towel and iron it using the correct heat setting for your fabric.

8. Rinse with cold water and use away!

"The LORD will guide you always; he will satisfy your needs in a sun-scorched land and will strengthen your frame. You will be like a well-watered garden, like a spring whose waters never fail."

Isaiah 58:11

✳ God's *Provision*

I AM A DEVOTED PLANT LADY. And by devoted, I mean that I can't for the life of me keep any plants alive, but I try incredibly hard to do so. I have dreamed of having a glorious garden like those of the Smithsonian and the beautiful Keukenhof Gardens in Lisse, the Netherlands. I would love to see hundreds of varieties of plants and vibrant colors popping in every direction, as far as the eye can see.

Alas, somewhat knowing my limitations, I settle for some potted plants, shrubs, and bushes from the local hardware store. When I bring them home, I tend to the plants, I talk to them, and I check their soil twice daily, all with the hope of growing them into their beautiful full potential. But a few weeks in, after some hot days and a long weekend away, the plants begin to look sad. Leaves are limp, blooms have ceased, and branches are weeping. What am I doing wrong? I begin to overobsess. I look at Google; I shop on Amazon; I troubleshoot. I pour on products, trim their limbs, and stare out my window, willing them to be as healthy as the day I brought them home. But nothing works. A month later, my husband sneaks them into the yard waste one by one.

The good news? My heart is in the right place, and I always have another season to try again.

The even better news? God knows what He is doing with us in every season.

We don't have to worry about His plan or whether He will provide what we need to reach our potential. He has known all along what we were meant to be, and He longs to be our source. We are never ignored or underwatered.

Our Heavenly Father doesn't take days off from His care for us. He is just
what we need when we need it.

Craft: Abstract Painted Flowerpots

MATERIALS

Terra-cotta plant pot
Variety of acrylic paint colors
Paintbrushes: two-inch and fan
Your favorite real or faux plant
Mod Podge
Whitewash *(optional)*

INSTRUCTIONS

1. Clean the surface of your terra-cotta pot. (I recommend painting the pot with a quick whitewash for a brighter, fresher background.)

2. Pour your choice of acrylic paints onto a paint plate or palette.

3. Beginning with one color, take a two-inch paintbrush and paint a block stripe of two to three inches with a sideways stroke in various places around the pot, leaving empty spaces that can be filled in with other colors.

4. Choose another color and continue with a sideways stroke in some of the empty spaces around the pot.

5. Use as many colors as possible, and repeat step three until the pot is mostly covered in blocks of color.

6. Gently dip a fan brush in white paint and lightly blend color blocks together with more sideways strokes.

7. Cover with a clear coat of Mod Podge to protect the paint.

8. Add your favorite plant.

Strength in *God's Word*

"For it is God who works in you to will and to act in order to fulfill his good purpose. Do everything without grumbling or arguing, so that you may become blameless and pure, 'children of God without fault in a warped and crooked generation.' Then you will shine among them like stars in the sky."

Philippians 2:13–15

❧Strength in
God's Word

I LOVE HOW MANY TIMES the phrase "children of God" is mentioned in the Bible. It reminds me that in our faith walk, it is helpful to dial back to when we were children and things were simpler, more believable, and almost more doable. When I was in the middle of an adventure at Washington, D.C.'s International Spy Museum, my children were running about with their little badges with secret spy names, decoding messages, and learning all about the history of espionage. Suddenly, I heard the ever-so-often-cried, "Mommy, look at me! Mommy, come here and look! Moooooommmmmy!" I quickly turned the corner to find my eight-year-old hanging by her fingers on an extremely high horizontal pole. I looked on the adjacent wall to see a red timer ticking away. She had reached twenty seconds and was still going! I was very impressed. She hung on for another nine seconds, almost making the full thirty seconds. After she flopped down on the ground, I gave her a huge hug and applauded her incredible efforts. We then sat on the ground, fascinated by the trial, and watched person after person attempt this great feat. And do you know who did an incredible job? The children!

We watched many adults and teens get up and wrestle with gravity. The biggest challenge came when the technician hit a button and the pole began to shake, resembling a gust of wind. Inevitably, the grown-ups would begin to squirm and adjust their grip, ultimately loosening their original trusted solid hold. Barely hanging on, they would soon fall flat on their backs (usually with an "oof" sound). There was something amazing and inspiring about a child simply hanging there, giving it their all, innocently believing that when the struggle arose and their grip slipped, a loving parent would swoop in and provide the necessary strength for them to keep holding on. When it was time to fall, the child let go, as if always safe. With a proud smile, they'd say, "I wanna do that again!"

Jesus referred to those following him and those listening to his stories as "children of God," and He guided them. Those who persevere tend to be young at heart—steadfast in their faith and trusting not in their own strength but in God, who keeps them up when they grow weary.

We tend to fight and wrestle with things as we grow older. If we can instead hold out an innocent hand and reach for a stronger hand, our battles might not seem so bleak and unachievable.

You have a great purpose! So when life feels heavy and you feel like you can't go on, remember He is always there. And you are always being held.

Craft: Mini Decoupage Floral Magnets

MATERIALS

Round magnets
Fabric or paper flowers
Mod Podge
Sponge brush

INSTRUCTIONS

1. You can trim your flowers to your desired size prior to starting the craft.

2. Use your sponge brush to cover the magnet with a thick layer of Mod Podge.

3. Place your paper or fabric flower onto the glue layer.

4. Hold your paper or fabric flower down firmly and then add another thick layer of Mod Podge. It's okay if the fabric flower petals keep popping up from the glue. They will firm up once the glue is dry and will give your magnet a little depth.

5. Lay your magnets flat to dry completely.

Never-Ending Light

"The city does not need the sun or the moon
to shine on it, for the glory of God gives it
light, and the Lamb is its lamp."

Revelations 21:23

✤ *Never-Ending* Light

ONE NIGHT, MY DAUGHTER ASKED FOR MY HELP with the newest addition to her princess tent: several strands of fairy lights. I quickly agreed, thinking there might be a snag or two in some of the strands. However, what she handed me was a large knotted ball of a thousand teeny-tiny twisted lights. I looked at her with wild eyes, asking how on earth they ever managed to get that way. She simply shrugged her shoulders, thanked me, and walked away smiling.

So, I got started.

At first, I would pick a strand and try to follow it through the knotted mess, attempting to unfasten it from its surrounding chaos. And just when I thought I was making headway, I'd realize I had somehow switched to another strand and was making things worse. I contemplated giving up. But as I looked across the room, I noticed the beautiful flickering of a brightly glowing candle. It was then that I had my moment of clarity.

I picked up a plastic end and turned on its switch. This illuminated only one single fairy light strand. And now, through the darkness, chaos, twists, and turns, I could finally see where I was going.

It still took me a while, but I was eventually able to untangle all seven strands of teeny-tiny lights. My fingers and eyes hurt, but my heart was warmed by the words I kept repeating to myself as I worked: "Just follow the light . . ." In the Book of Revelation, John wrote about this and the vision of a beautiful, bright city with no need for lamps, the sun, or the moon: all radiance coming from above, streaming straight from God's great glory. What a vision!

God doesn't want us to feel entangled and twisted up in all the wicked ways of this world.

He sent His Son to be the light and to shine through the chaos and confusion so we can be sure of where He wants us to go. It may be a different destination than we originally anticipated, but we can know He is always guiding us.

So, next time you find yourself knotted up or struggling to find your way through the darkness, remember the never-ending guiding light that is your Savior. Look for it; reach for it; follow it. It will always lead you home.

Craft: Wooden Candle Holder

MATERIALS

Six-inch diameter birch disk
Package of small birch pieces
Candle
Hot glue gun or wood glue (optional if you want yours to be attached permanently)

INSTRUCTIONS

1. Stack four small birch pieces on top of each other.

2. Repeat to make four stacks total.

3. Put the large birch disk on top, pushing the four stacks close together under the middle of the disk and making sure it's level.

4. Glue all the pieces together (optional).

5. Finish with a pretty candle!

CRAFT: Woven Keychains

The Keys
of Teaching

"I will give you the keys of the kingdom of heaven; whatever you bind on earth will be bound in heaven, and whatever you loose on earth will be loosed in heaven."

Matthew 16:19

The Keys
of Teaching

WHEN IT WAS TIME TO CHOOSE where my daughter would go to kindergarten, my heart was a mess. She had attended a beautiful faith-filled preschool, where there were prayers over goldfish crackers, a chapel, and a common Heavenly goal in her education. I was convinced the next piece in the puzzle was her attendance at a Catholic school where I was leading a weekly Bible study. I wanted her to be with all the other families I had grown close to, and I wanted her to be surrounded by all the things that had supported her in previous years.

Things did not go as planned, and I was having the hardest time understanding why God wouldn't just pave the way for her education within this faith-filled school. One Sunday at church, I heard this verse from Matthew as part of a wonderful sermon about discipleship. My pastor went on to tell us how the keys to God's kingdom are in our hands. They are a gift from our loving Heavenly Father, and what we do with them is up to us. Will we clutch the keys close to our hearts and invite others in, sharing God's word with everyone we meet? Will we grab the keys and simply hide them deep down in our pockets? Or will we hold tight to the keys on some days, all the while trying our hardest to dictate life's wheres, whens, whys, and hows?

I left church that morning with an inkling of what God might be trying to teach me. He wanted me to let go and let Him work His magic within my daughter. He loves her more than I could ever imagine and will be with her no matter where she hangs her backpack. The following weeks brought clarity and a newfound understanding of the opportunity and blessing it would be for my daughter to share her light with those in our neighborhood public school.

God needs us to be the eyes and ears of the gospel in our words and actions.

We are to share His kingdom with the world. Sometimes, He leads us far away from familiarity and into the wilderness in the hope that we will let go of our surroundings and fully rely on Him. With His guidance, He will fill our days and nights with chances to look up and follow Him.

Craft: Woven Keychains

MATERIALS

Beads in a variety of colors, shapes, and sizes
Bracelet string
Yarn in your favorite colors
Keychain rings

INSTRUCTIONS

1. Cut about a six- to eight-inch length of bracelet string.

2. Tie a knot around the keychain ring with one end of your bracelet string.

3. String four to six beads in your desired pattern.

4. Tie a knot in the end after the last bead. Set the beads aside..

5. To make the tassel, wrap the yarn around four fingers on one hand about ten times. Remove the yarn from your hand, keeping the circle form, and cut it free from the large yarn skein. Cut a small piece of new yarn and tie it around the top of the yarn circle, bundling the strands together. Now, cut the bottom part of the yarn circle. This should create hanging strands. Almost done! Wrap a foot-long piece of new yarn around the outside of the bunch of yarn, about an inch down from the top, creating a little tassel head. Wrap the yarn around a few times and tie it in a double knot. Lastly, take the end of your beaded piece and fasten it through the top of the tassel.

Purpose
and Plan

"Do not conform to the pattern of this world, but be transformed by the renewing of your mind. Then you will be able to test and approve what God's will is—his good, pleasing and perfect will."

Romans 12:2

Purpose
and Plan

DURING THE LAST CHURCH service before the March 2020 COVID-19 shutdown, my pastor looked at his congregation and begged us to treat the next day as we would any other day. It was a hard thing for many people to wrap their heads around, with their kids staying home from school and many companies closed and work suspended. No one quite knew how to react. But the words I heard that day gave me a mission: not to react but to simply act as God was calling me to do. I took my pastor's marching orders very much to heart and worked through the night until the wee hours of the morning—printing, cutting, drawing, and making. When the next morning arrived, I was ready.

The girls and I had our very first Bible & Breakfast since no one had to race off to catch a bus. After that, we went on a brisk walk to get the blood flowing, and then we started school at home with yours truly as the teacher. Little did I know that those months spent learning, exploring, and renewing our minds inside our little home, while the world outside was confused and chaotic, would prepare me for the next school year when I bravely took the role of lead teacher in a homeschool co-op.

Looking back on that simple Sunday, sitting in church with my ears open and my heart unsure, I can see now that God was asking me to just go. Not to a physical place on a map but in the direction of His will: His plan for me. Dusting off my teaching hat after a hiatus of more than a decade was one of the most rewarding things I've ever done. And our time together was truly the best year my family has ever had.

When you hear His gentle voice calling you to step out of your comfort zone and away from the world's pattern, transformation awaits.

He doesn't call the equipped, but
He will equip the called.

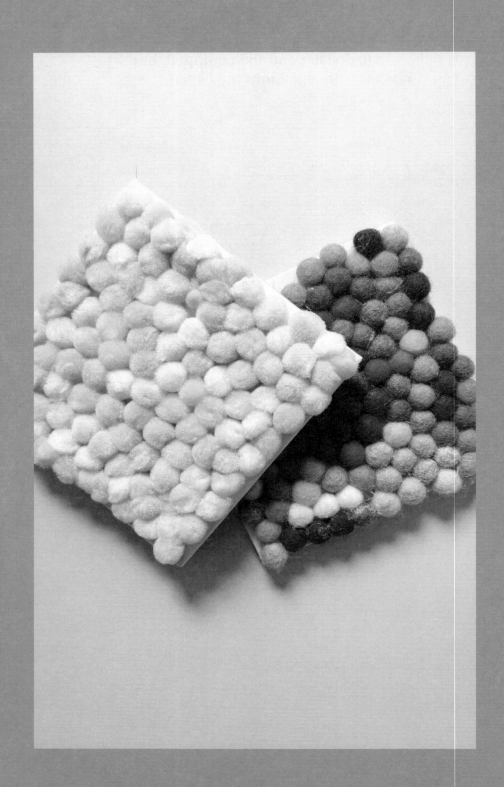

Craft: Cozy Pom-Pom Coasters

MATERIALS

One tile (*I used a four-inch square tile for this project; single tile samples can often be purchased at home improvement stores or in small packs at craft stores.*)
Mod Podge
Sponge brush
Small pom-poms
Cardstock
Furniture sliders (*optional*)

INSTRUCTIONS

1. Place the tile on top of the cardstock and trace around the edges. Cut out the outline to give you a square of cardstock the same size as the tile.

2. Use your sponge brush to glue the cardstock onto the top of the tile with the Mod Podge.

3. Allow to dry.

4. Add a generous amount of Mod Podge over the cardstock on the tile, and then spread the pom-poms all over it, pushing them closely together with your fingers to make a tight fit and cover the entire coaster.

5. Allow to dry completely before using.

Crown
of Believers

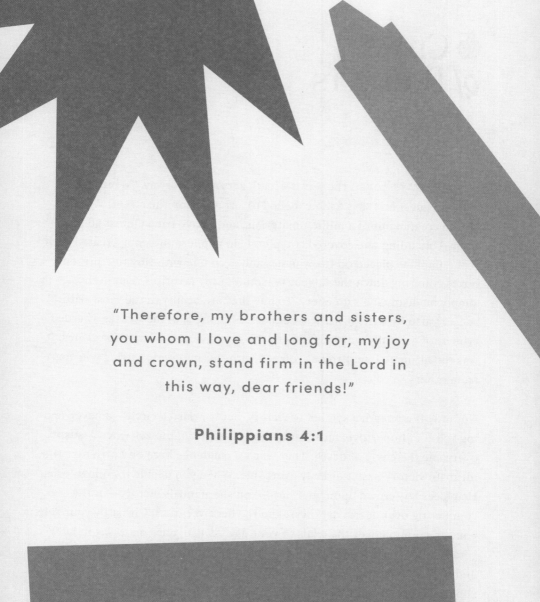

"Therefore, my brothers and sisters, you whom I love and long for, my joy and crown, stand firm in the Lord in this way, dear friends!"

Philippians 4:1

Crown
of Believers

I HAVE ALWAYS LOVED the way a wreath adorns a doorway. To me, it welcomes a guest and says a kind "hello" to a traveler on the street. Wreaths can be created out of a million materials, and I have tried almost all of them—including one covered completely in peppermints, one created with real pumpkins placed on fuzzy moss, and even one with tiny tied present boxes counting down the Advent season. But my favorites remain those simply made of God's greenery. To me, they are beauty in the most natural sense. I also love the historical connection. Long ago, the Greeks awarded crowns of carefully woven greens to the proud victors of races or games. It was the ultimate honor to be crowned with this greenery, setting you apart from others.

Not only is a wreath a symbol of victory, but it is also a circle—a never-ending spiral of hope, love, faith, and promises that symbolizes when Jesus overcame the curse of death. There isn't a challenge here on Earth that His ultimate victory hasn't already overcome. When you decide to follow Jesus, He places His crown upon your head. You share in His victory—in His conquering over death, darkness, and the deceiver. With Christ by your side, you can triumph over the trials of your day. As Paul goes on to say in later verses in this chapter, his last letter to the Philippians: "Finally, brothers and sisters, whatever is true, whatever is noble, whatever is right, whatever is pure, whatever is lovely, whatever is admirable—if anything is excellent or praiseworthy—think about such things. Whatever you have learned or received or heard from me or seen in me—put it into practice. And the God of peace will be with you" (Philippians 4:8–9).

What encouragement Paul gives his audience as he says goodbye: to grab hold of the joy and the crown that we have been given and then to try to walk in the path of truth, nobility, purity, loveliness, and excellence, and then to practice these things in our daily lives.

<blockquote>Heaven is cheering you on—as loud and uplifting as a stadium praising a victor.</blockquote>

Now, go out into this world with hope in your heart and your head and your crown held high.

Craft: Eucalyptus Door Wreath

MATERIALS

Wreath form *(I recommend either a gold hoop, grapevine, or wooden beaded form. I chose a wooden beaded form for this project.)*
Eucalyptus leaves or part of a garland
Wooden "hello" sign
Floral wire
Glue dots or double-sided tape

INSTRUCTIONS

1. Cut several two-inch pieces of the floral wire.

2. Grab the eucalyptus leaves and place them around the wreath form in your desired location.

3. Secure the leaves to the wreath form with floral wire in two to three places.

4. Decide the placement of your "hello" sign and secure it to the eucalyptus leaves using glue dots or double-sided tape.

✳ Unseen
Adornments

"Your beauty should not come from outward adornment, such as elaborate hairstyles and the wearing of gold jewelry or fine clothes. Rather, it should be that of your inner self, the unfading beauty of a gentle and quiet spirit, which is of great worth in God's sight."

1 Peter 3:3—4

Unseen
Adornments

I WAS PRIVILEGED one Sunday morning to sit at a table and represent my Bible study for a "meet and greet" outside the church. I was paired with a darling young woman, whom I had become friends with over the course of her first session. We chatted for a long time between the different masses, serenaded by faint organ music and the hustle and bustle of the busy sidewalk. She was originally from Italy, where I had traveled in my college days. I was fascinated by her stories of growing up in such a different culture, how she met her husband, and what she filled her days with as an energetic young woman in the D.C. area. That morning, I asked why she had chosen our Bible study and what had ultimately compelled her to come back after the initial open house event. I will never forget her response.

She said whenever she went to the different city social events, she worried. She worried about what to wear, what she should say, and whether she would have anything in common with the other people there. When she bravely walked into our Bible study for the first time, she didn't have a worry. She knew that no matter what she wore or what she said, she had one very important thing in common with the ladies in that room—we all loved God.

In that moment, my sweet friend knew that God sees our hearts.

He looks through the expensive clothes, past the good and bad hair days, and straight into what counts—a love for Him that is an unfading beauty. May this be of comfort to you on your best days, as well as on those when you don't feel your best. Your Heavenly Father sees your inner self.

Craft: Beaded Ornaments

MATERIALS

Circular or square wooden beads
Gold wire
Cardstock
Circular wooden sign disks or printed circular signs
Jute string
Small pieces of greenery
Scissors and craft glue or hot glue

INSTRUCTIONS

1. Glue your wooden circle or printed circle onto the cardstock.

2. Leave a one-inch border around the circle as you cut the cardstock. Set aside.

3. Take your gold wire and string the beads, checking the measurement and circumference to see how many are needed to create a border around your wooden or printed circle.

4. Add a line of glue around the cardstock border of the circle and press your wired beads down, creating an ornamental frame.

5. Finish by adding some greenery and a jute bow with your glue.

➜ Clothing Us *in* His Righteousness

"I delight greatly in the LORD;
my soul rejoices in my God. For he has
clothed me with garments of salvation and
arrayed me in a robe of his righteousness,
as a bridegroom adorns his head like a
priest, and as a bride adorns herself
with her jewels."

Isaiah 61:10

Clothing Us *in* His Righteousness

CONFESSION: I AM DANGEROUS when I shop in a home department store. I am extremely kind and courteous to fellow shoppers, but I always walk away with way more than I planned.

Last week, I went in for a salad bowl. I came out with pillows, a lamp, a throw, a matching rug, and a large six-by-six foot abstract painting. How did that happen?

I'll tell you what happens: I forget what I have, and I completely focus on what I want, or what I think I want. So, when a stylish lamp catches my eye, I innocently place it in my cart, losing all sense of the eleven lamps I already have in every corner of my home. I continue down the aisles, blissfully placing multiple lamp-matching items into my cart. I then go through the checkout with enough items to fill a room but, alas, no salad bowl.

At the heart of this problem is my constant need for things.

We are pushed to believe that surrounding ourselves with material comforts, from lamps and pillows to sweatpants and steamy lattes, will quench our restless hearts and end the searching. But the reality is we are hardwired to only be satisfied by a relationship with Jesus. The danger comes when we cover this truth with many superficial layers and end up confused, cluttered, and constantly coming up short of how we are meant to live.

We can break this cycle by focusing on Truth. When was the last time you used the words "delight" or "rejoice"? To be honest, I was both delighted and rejoicing as I brought home my fabulous newest finds from the shopping trip. But it all quickly faded as my dog chewed on the pillows, the baby spilled juice on the throw, crayon marks appeared on the rug, and the bulb burned out in the lamp. Those feelings simply don't last.

Isaiah wants to remind us that when we shift our focus to what we already have in Christ, our Savior, believing that He is enough, we are clothed in garments of salvation. No shopping trip required.

Craft: Paint Chip Garland

MATERIALS

Variety of paint chips in your desired colors *(two of each specific color)*
Circle hole punch *(I used a one-inch hole punch for this project.)*
Twine
Tacky glue

INSTRUCTIONS

1. Decide on your color scheme(s).

2. Use the hole punch to cut out two circles of each hue.

3. Repeat with all the colors that you would like on your garland.

4. Pick the colors that you want on your garland and glue the circles closely together on the twine in the order you prefer.

5. Allow it to dry.

6. Flip the garland over and add the matching colored circles to the back.

7. Hang and enjoy!

Waiting *for* the Lord

"Wait for the LORD;
be strong and take heart
and wait for the LORD."

Psalm 27:14

# Waiting *for* the Lord

I BELIEVE GOD may give us home renovations in life to tame our ever-impatient hearts and build some very necessary faith for the journey ahead. My family had a simple plan to quickly update our upstairs bathroom—the one our three oldest daughters use. We had hoped that by upgrading to double sinks, double mirrors, more storage, and a shiny new shower, the arguments and bickering might come to a halt. While that is certainly a pipe dream for any parent, God had other plans. He decided to take the heat off the girls' behavior and put my own heart under the microscope.

Each new day of the small renovation brought news that something else had gone wrong, requiring additional work and extra time. I was quickly losing patience. Our baby was in a temporary nursery in the back room of the basement, not napping, while my three older girls were busy using (and destroying) my bathroom every morning and night, and the constant noise through the walls was becoming deafening. Throughout the process, I learned that I need a lot of God's help in the patience department.

How can we find happiness and calm amid trials?
What can we focus on when timelines linger
and the end seems nowhere in sight?

The Psalmist states that the keys to successful steadfastness are being strong and taking heart. In other words, be confident, positive, comforted, and encouraged. I learned that the term "take heart" originates from the Bible and is mentioned many times throughout the Bible when there are questions, tribulations, and situations in disarray. One of the times it is mentioned is when our dear Jesus, speaking to his disciples on Maundy Thursday, foretold of His Passion and pain: "I have told you these things, so that in me you may have peace. In this world you will have trouble. But take heart! I have overcome the world" (John 16:33). Notice that he uses the words "take heart" amid his pain. Jesus is sitting with an intimate gathering, encouraging His closest friends and followers to not focus on the "whys" and "why nots" and all they cannot understand at that moment. Instead, He guides them to shift their focus to trusting in His promises and pressing on until the end. Because it will be good.

So, if I can learn to wait for serenity from double sinks with waterfall faucets, I can learn to wait on the promises of the Lord. Because He is good.

Craft: Sun Prints

MATERIALS

Cyanotype paper
Small flowers and plants
Sun
Picture frame

INSTRUCTIONS

1. Pick your flowers and plants. Note that the more intricate and delicate the details on the plant, the more the sun will shine through, creating a better X-ray effect.

2. Away from direct sunlight, arrange your flowers and plants in your desired pattern and position directly onto the cyanotype paper.

3. Lay your paper in a very sunny (and preferably not windy!) spot for approximately five minutes. When it is ready, the paper should appear lighter in color.

4. Bring the paper inside and remove the flowers and plants. You should see dark images of the flowers and plants on the paper.

5. Run it under cold water until the paper turns blue and the shadows turn white.

6. Allow to dry completely in a cool place.

7. Display and enjoy!

In *God's* Thoughts

"How precious to me are your thoughts,
God! How vast is the sum of them!"

Psalm 139:17

# In *God's* Thoughts

I FIND IT SO HARD TO BE SATISFIED with any photos of myself. I am super critical, constantly overanalyzing, and seem to have a gift for finding even the slightest imperfections within a photograph. When we had annual family portraits taken during our beach vacation, my toddler threw a complete tantrum almost the whole time while I fought the wind from messing up my hair, battled the waves that crashed onto my long dress, and prayed there would be one good photo choice for a future Christmas card. I left the session thinking that if we walked away with beautiful photos of my precious children, I would be a happy camper. And we sure did. Truth be told, my favorite photo to date is the one that captured my toddler's meltdown in all its glory while she sat in the sand with her beautiful, sweetly smiling sisters. It's a memory I will cherish forever.

Psalm 139 is possibly the most heartfelt collection of words illustrating how much God truly loves us and knows us. Famous verses include ". . . you knit me together in my mother's womb" (Psalm 139:13) and "I praise you because I am fearfully and wonderfully made" (Psalm 139:14). Phrases from this psalm have been turned into cards, baby blankets, picture books, and artwork for walls. Why? Because they are wonderful reminders of how much we are thought of by our Heavenly Father.

When I read this verse originally, I did not quite understand the magnitude of the words "your thoughts." "How precious it is, Lord, to realize that you are thinking about me constantly! I can't even count how many times a day your thoughts turn toward me. And when I waken in the morning, you are still thinking of me!" (Psalm 139:17–18 The Living Bible). I absolutely love this translation. It brings to life the reality that God is always thinking of us. Always! He's not quickly flipping through an album and favoriting only those images where we look picture-perfect. Rather, no matter what we are doing—meltdowns and all—we are constantly in the mind of the Maker of the world. Our Maker.

He sees us. He knows us. He loves us.

After reading this verse, I imagined never-ending hallways vastly lined with picture frames: one for each moment of our lives. Walk through it in your mind. Stop and gaze at those moments. Now, look even closer. He is there in them all. You are precious to Him, and He hasn't missed a thing.

Craft: Straw Picture Frames

MATERIALS

Picture frame
Paper straws in your desired color(s)
Scissors and craft glue or hot glue
Ruler

INSTRUCTIONS

1. Pick a place on your picture frame to start and select your first paper straw. Hold the straw up to measure it against the frame and cut it to the correct size.

2. Glue the straw piece directly onto your frame.

3. Depending on the size and style of your frame, continue adding straw pieces until the entire frame is covered.

4. Pop in your favorite picture and enjoy!

God's
Deliverance

"I removed the burden from their shoulders;
their hands were set free from the basket.
In your distress you called and I rescued
you, I answered you out of a thundercloud;
I tested you at the waters of Meribah."

Psalm 81:6–7
(NIV)

God's
Deliverance

I WILL NEVER FORGET THE TIME I rescued my kindergarten class from a spider. This was not just any spider. It was a big, jumpy, make-your-skin-crawl-when-you-look-at-it kind of spider. The children at the front of the room started whispering and pointing, and within seconds, they were all screaming and hopping up on desks. I was in the middle of a reading group in the back of the room and had no idea what all the commotion was about. So, I sternly asked the children to quiet down and behave themselves.

As the screaming turned to shrieking, one child ran up to me, tugged on my dress, and asked me to please help. I realized how powerless they all felt. I calmly grabbed a pile of paper towels from the sink area and hunched close to the spider. At that point, it had become so quiet in the room that I think I could hear the spider breathing. I grabbed the spider with the paper towels and flushed it down the toilet. Cheering erupted!

I am truly one hundred percent petrified of all things that creep and crawl. Even the littlest ones. So it's amazing to think how brave I was at that very moment. And do you know why? I had help. Would I have seized that disgusting creature bare-handed? Oh, dear heavens, no. The plethora of paper towels between me and my spider-sized fear was enough to safeguard me through the whole ordeal. And I appeared ever so heroic to my doting room of six-year-olds.

We are not meant to go through life petrified or weighed down by our daily burdens.

We have help—an advocate. One who walks before us, with us, protecting us from distress. God wants to come between us and our problems. These are reassuring words: "I removed the burden from their shoulders; their hands were set free from the basket."

A commentary I read regarding this verse speaks of the basket being filled with clay that was meant to be turned into bricks. Basically, arms full of important stuff. Can you relate? To me, the most important part of this verse comes right before the rescue. "In your distress you called . . ." Knowing we need rescuing doesn't solve our problems, but it's certainly a step in the right direction. We also need to reach up and call for assistance to lighten our loads and for His shield and safeguarding in all our storms of life.

Craft: Rope Basket with Handles

MATERIALS

Metal bucket
Thick rope
Scissors
Craft glue or hot glue

INSTRUCTIONS

1. Flip the bucket over so the bottom is facing up.

2. Starting at the bottom, lay a line of glue about six inches long.

3. Follow quickly by laying the rope directly on top of the glue, pressing down, and doing your best to make a straight line.

4. Repeat steps two and three until you reach two inches below the top of the bucket.

5. Cut a set of handles of your desired length from the rope.

6. Using your glue and pressing firmly, set a handle on each side of the bucket.

7. Finish wrapping the rope around the remaining two inches of the bucket, going over the place where you attached the handles and securing and hiding any ends.

8. Fill with whatever you would like and marvel at what you made!

➜ Fixing Our Eyes
on God's Word

"Teach them to your children, talking about them when you sit at home and when you walk along the road, when you lie down and when you get up. Write them on the door-frames of your houses and on your gates, so that your days and the days of your children may be many in the land the LORD swore to give your ancestors, as many as the days that the heavens are above the earth."

Deuteronomy 11:19–21

➜ Fixing Our Eyes
on God's Word

I WILL NEVER FORGET THE NIGHT my daughter was having terrible trouble with some scary thoughts and couldn't quite fall asleep. She had come down to our living room many times throughout the night. Each time, we sent her back up with a different strategy to help her settle. First, we gave her a cup of warm milk. Then, we made sure she had all her special blankets and favorite stuffed animals close by. Next, we told her a few stories to take her mind off the bad thoughts. Nothing worked.

It occurred to me that we should be getting to the root of the problem, not just comforting her on the outside. So, I sat on her bed, and we talked about how the devil works. I told her about his lies, his deception, and his love of fear and worry. She was fascinated to hear all about it. And then she asked the most important question of all: "Mom, how do I fight the devil?"

If anything had prepared me for this question at this very moment, it was my many years of Bible study. Each lesson brought more knowledge of different Bible verses into my heart—and many had made it onto the walls of our home. And it was exactly what was needed.

I told her that my most recent study had a section in the back of the book called the "I declares." The author, Lisa Brenninkmeyer, wrote these verses in her 2017 book, *Fearless and Free*, to declare truths while battling the sneaky lies of the deceiver.

My daughter's eyes lit up, and she asked, "Mom, can we try it?"

"Oh, my darling, most certainly yes," I quickly replied.

Right then and there, we stood up to Satan. We declared the biblical truths to battle head-to-head with his falsehoods. When she felt like a failure, we took inspiration from 2 Corinthians 12:10 and declared, "When I am weak, you are strong within me." When she heard that God had forgotten her, we repeated: "The steadfast love of the LORD never ceases; his mercies never come to an end; they are new every morning; great is your faithfulness" (Lamentations 3:22–23 English Standard Version).

One by one, we squashed the lies and replaced them with His Word. And there is nothing that His Word won't conquer.

My daughter eventually fell asleep with a cup of cold milk and her extra-loved bears nearby, but she didn't really need any of those things. She needed to be blanketed in the truth. When you feel that you are under attack or in the middle of a battle, resist the temptation to only comfort and shield your body. You need to go after the real attack, the one on your heart and soul. Grab hold of the bold, beautiful truths told to you within the pages of the Bible, "talking about them when you sit at home" and writing them "on the doorframes of your houses and on your gates" so that you are ready to fight. Put a verse as the background on your phone, use one as a bookmark in the book you are reading, pin one up on your kitchen cupboard, or have it as a pretty Pinterest poster on your wall. Keep the words close, and keep Him even closer.

Take a moment to reflect on these truths below.

_____

_____

_____

_____

_____

_____

_____

_____

_____

_____

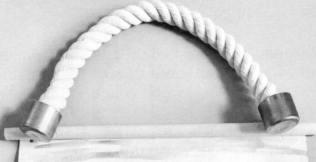

When you
go through
deep waters,
I will be
with you.

Isaiah 43:2

Craft: Verse Wall Hanging

MATERIALS

Your favorite Bible verse printed on watercolor paper
Watercolor set and water
Two dowel rods
Rope
Set of copper pipe ends
Hot glue gun
Pocket knife or small craft saw

INSTRUCTIONS

1. Decorate your Bible verse with watercolor paint.

2. Let it dry.

3. Line up your dowel rods with your paper, marking two to three inches further out from both sides of the paper.

4. Use a pocket knife or small craft saw to cut the dowel rods.

5. Measure out your rope and glue the copper ends onto the ends of the rope.

6. Hot glue the copper ends to the left and right of the top dowel rod.

7. Hang and enjoy!

✳ Wisdom *and* Understanding

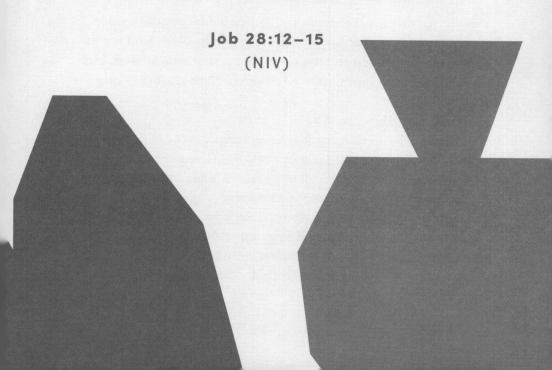

"But where can wisdom be found?
Where does understanding dwell?
No mortal comprehends its worth;
it cannot be found in the land of the living.
The deep says, 'It is not in me';
the sea says, 'It is not with me.'
It cannot be bought with the finest gold,
nor can its price be weighed out in silver."

Job 28:12–15
(NIV)

✳ Wisdom *and* Understanding

MY FATHER IS AN INCREDIBLE STORYTELLER. He has this amazing gift of wrapping you into every word while he speaks. He would have us laughing, crying, and feeling every emotion from beginning to end. I remember sitting on our couch as a child, curled up and waiting for him to come home with more anecdotes from his day. But if I remember correctly, my favorite ones were the stories of his past, the ones he was passing down from the life lessons he learned with his father, mother, sisters, neighbors, and school friends.

I treasured those stories and begged for more. Not only were they entertaining, but they also taught me that through tough trials, there is always an opportunity to gain wisdom. There's always a chance to trust in God's providence, to believe that everything will turn out well in the end.

This certainly rang true observing my father; his age brought wisdom. I'm still working on that part myself. I keep getting older, but I am still making the same mistakes. I can see it now; in my future memoir, I will have ninety-nine chapters, all titled, "Oops . . . I did it again!" I pray I'll get there someday.

What I have come to understand is the difference between knowledge and wisdom. While knowledge is gathered from learning and experience, wisdom is the ability to put it all into practice. I feel many of us can say we have acquired lots of knowledge and information but often have trouble putting it into play. In a world where, at any time, we can press a button and have our questions answered by an automated assistant or get GPS to recalculate our directions in an instant, it can be hard to understand that God's wisdom works a little differently. It comes to us when we seek it, but not always within our preferred timeframe, and it might not look exactly like our own well-planned blueprints.

In the verse on page 81, Job is debating with friends about where true wisdom originates. He writes that it is not in the deep or the sea, cannot be bought with silver or gold, and "cannot be found in the land of the living." I feel like the next line should read, "nor found on the internet or a phone." So, what is Job saying here? I believe he's arguing that the kind of wisdom that answers tough questions—such as "why?" or "when?" or "how come?" —is not found here on Earth. It rests in God's hands. True surrender in our lives comes when we rely fully on His answers in His time. Easier said than done, for sure.

We are all a work in progress.

And just as a wise and loving father is always ready to share another valuable story to help us walk a little wiser, so will our Heavenly Maker take the time to make all things good in our own story. Sometimes, all we need to do is wait, and then just curl up and listen closely.

_____

_____

_____

_____

_____

_____

_____

_____

_____

_____

_____

_____

_____

Craft: Upcycled Vases

MATERIALS

Vases of varying sizes
Chalk paint *(in white and black)*
Baking soda
Mod Podge
Paintbrush
Washi tape

INSTRUCTIONS

1. Wash your vases, cleaning them of any dust or dirt.

2. Cover your vases with a layer of Mod Podge and let them dry.

3. Once dried, mix one part white chalk paint with one part baking soda until the paint is slightly fluffy.

4. Apply a layer of white paint on the top three-quarters of one of the vases.

5. Apply a layer of white paint to the bottom three-quarters of the other vase.

6. Let the vases dry.

7. Repeat steps three through six with the black chalk paint and cover the remaining quarter of each vase.

8. Continue painting alternately until each vase is covered completely, usually two or three layers.

9. Finish by placing your favorite washi tape where the paint colors meet. (This was my secret to not stressing over painting perfectly straight lines!)

Wearing Mercy *and* Truth

"Let love and faithfulness never leave you; bind them around your neck, write them on the tablet of your heart."

Proverbs 3:3

🝰 Wearing Mercy *and* Truth

I WAS SITTING CRISSCROSS on my bed one night, detangling a knot in the chain of one of my favorite necklaces. I was trying hard to pinch one end and pull it away from the other. After some time—my vision blurring and my fingers growing tired—I was able to unknot the chain. But this didn't happen how I thought it would. Instead of working at the knot itself and pulling in different directions, I pushed the two opposite sides of the chain closer together, gently forcing the tiny tangle to eventually loosen.

Relationships are a lot like chains on your favorite necklace. They also take a lot of work to keep straight, and sometimes those unpleasant kinks and knots show up. A wonderful speaker said something I pray will always stick with me. He started with the well-known idea that two people in a relationship need to both give an equal fifty percent, totaling one hundred, to really make things work. He then went on to ask the room what happens if one of the people involved can't give their fifty percent. They could be too tired, weary, overworked, underappreciated, hurt, or a variety of other possible reasons. What happens then? How can you reach that goal of one hundred percent? He challenged the members of the audience to "always give one hundred percent." There may be times when your partner, friend, coworker, or child is unable to lift the load. Perhaps they're having a bad day and can only give a maximum of twenty percent. But if you still give everything you've got, together you'll reach a strong and mighty one hundred and twenty percent.

Now, you might be asking how that's even possible when you are sometimes struggling yourself. Remember that you have an ever-present advocate in your corner.

The Holy Spirit brings the love, joy, peace, patience, kindness, goodness, and other fruits needed to get through. All we need to do is ask.

Instead of pulling away in fear or worry, resentment or anger, pray for positivity and to be pushed in love toward the people in your life.

Is there a relationship in your life that feels tied up in knots? Give that extra effort, surpass expectations, abound with faithfulness and love, and I think you'll be surprised to see just how many of those hard knots come unraveled before your eyes.

Craft:
Simple Jewelry

MATERIALS

Necklace chain in your preferred length
A stone or a jewel
Jewelry wire
Jump ring
Pliers
Wire cutters

INSTRUCTIONS

1. Take your stone or jewel and wrap the wire around it as many times as needed to create the look you like.

2. Before snipping the wire, turn the stone over and create a small loop on the back. Then, wrap the wire around the bottom of the new loop once or twice more to secure the closed loop to the stone.

3. Using the pliers, open the jump ring and secure it to your wire loop.

4. Fasten the jump ring to your necklace chain.

5. Close the jump ring with the pliers.

6. Voilà!

Reflection of All the Good *from* God

"Anyone who listens to the word but does not do what it says is like someone who looks at his face in a mirror and, after looking at himself, goes away and immediately forgets what he looks like. But whoever looks intently into the perfect law that gives freedom, and continues in it—not forgetting what they have heard, but doing it—they will be blessed in what they do."

James 1:23–25

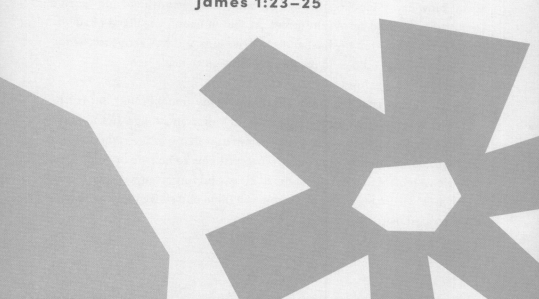

✼ Reflection of All the Good *from* God

ON OUR WAY HOME from my husband's family farm, we stopped to get his teeth cleaned. I know that sounds a bit silly, but he loves his family dentist. They had an opening, and we were going that way home, so it all made sense. Since we had a car full of kids, the plan was to let them play and hop around while my husband was in the dentist's office, and we would survive the time just fine. However, we had been driving through the small towns with an expired inspection sticker, and we were constantly fearful we would get pulled over and slapped with a hefty ticket. My husband directed me to lay low and stay in the parking lot. Approximately twenty minutes into the appointment, the kids were going wild. I had spotted a car wash two streetlights away, so I thought to myself, "How fun will this be for the kids? As a bonus, my husband will walk out with clean teeth and a clean car!"

I pulled out of the parking lot. All was going well—the kids were giddy with distraction, the car was getting cleaned, and a text arrived from my husband saying he was almost finished. Then, as we were going through the giant blow dryer, I looked through my super clean windshield and spotted a police car parked across the street. At that moment, I realized I had completely forgotten my husband's instructions and was about to pay for it—literally. And I did. And my husband was quite mad.

I'd like to blame that expensive afternoon on my "mom brain." But truthfully, I sometimes just forget things—even important things. In the Bible, James reminds us that when we work hard at walking in the right direction but act in a way that is contrary to what we know to be true or good, it's like we've looked in a mirror, stepped away, and forgotten what we look like. If we seek wisdom and guidance from the Bible and strive daily to be who God created us to be, we will be blessed.

God is very forgiving when we slip up. So come back to him, morning or night or in between, and remember who you were meant to be.

Craft: Raffia Mirror

MATERIALS

Raffia *(one package per mirror)*
Six-inch hoop
Six-inch mirror
Scissors
Ruler
Hot glue gun
Iron and dish towel

INSTRUCTIONS

1. Unravel the raffia from its package.

2. Starting with one cord at a time, collect a handful of raffia between your fingers and stretch it out to measure ten-inch strips.

3. Cut the strips and set them aside.

4. Repeat steps two and three until all the raffia is used.

5. Grab a handful of the cut raffia, put it between two layers of a dish towel, and iron it flat. Set it aside.

6. Repeat until all the raffia has been ironed.

7. Take 3-5 pieces of ironed raffia, stack them, and fold in half to form a loop. Place the folded raffia around the hoop and pull the loose ends through the loop to knot tightly.

8. Repeat step seven all the way around the hoop until the hoop is completely covered. Push the knots closely together as you work to create a fuller look and avoid any gaps.

9. Flip the raffia hoop over and, working quickly in a circle, add drops of hot glue directly on top of the knots. Then, while the glue is still hot, place your mirror face down in the middle of the hoop and press it onto the ring of hot glue.

10. Let it cool.

11. Hang and enjoy!

Loving *Our* Neighbors

"Love must be sincere. Hate what is evil; cling to what is good. Be devoted to one another in love. Honor one another above yourselves. Never be lacking in zeal, but keep your spiritual fervor, serving the Lord. Be joyful in hope, patient in affliction, faithful in prayer. Share with the Lord's people who are in need. Practice hospitality."

Romans 12:9–13

Loving *Our* Neighbors

GROWING UP IN A PREACHER'S HOME, right next to the church, meant we pretty much lived with an open-door policy. There were always people ringing our doorbell, tapping on the glass, or just stopping by. They were neighbors, church parishioners, strangers, and often homeless men and women—and my parents were abundantly caring to all. I would sometimes sit on the top steps of our large staircase, just out of sight but close enough to eavesdrop on the visit. If I didn't get a glimpse of the visitor when they first introduced themselves on the porch or when they walked in, I would listen intently to the conversation, trying to put a face, purpose, and back-story to the interaction. And it taught me something very important. People matter—all people.

One Thanksgiving, my mother put this belief into practice at our dining room table. Unlike previous years when our chairs were filled with extended family and an adopted grandmother or two from the parish, she decided to invite those who had no other place to be on this day of grat-itude. It's funny that I don't quite remember the names or faces of those who surrounded me that day, but I remember the feeling perfectly. It was a feeling of servitude and zeal. I was so excited to help create a beautiful tablescape and prepare delicious dishes that would satisfy our new guests. But moreover, it was a joy to have them with us in our home. There was a feeling of overwhelming thankfulness, like the day was supposed to feel. My family was given the gift of understanding our own blessings as our guests received much-needed care, warm food, and hospitality.

> I truly think that when we reach out and serve others, there is a deep connection to our Lord and Savior.

He has given us so many gifts and blessings. When we use these for His will, His purposes, or His people, I picture Him smiling down on us. Let us "cling to what is good," "be joyful in hope," and "share with the Lord's people who are in need." How can you serve someone today?

Craft: Farmhouse Tiered Tray

MATERIALS

Cake pan
Pie pan
Pizza pan
Two candle jars
Chalk paint and paintbrush
E6000 glue
Placemats

INSTRUCTIONS

1. Paint your three pans with chalk paint, allowing plenty of time to dry on the placemats before applying a second coat. (The best part about chalk paint and the farmhouse look is you don't need to be a master painter. When the metal of the pan shows through a bit, it creates a shabby chic, distressed look. Just go with it!)

2. Paint both the candle jars with chalk paint. They will need a few layers of paint to cover.

3. Starting with the painted pizza pan as the base, glue the first candle jar upside down onto the middle of the pizza pan.

4. Glue the bottom of the pie pan onto the top of the upside-down candle jar.

5. Add the second candle jar, upside down, to the middle of the pie pan and glue it on.

6. Finish by gluing the bottom of the cake pan on top of the second candle jar.

7. Add accessories and display!

✳ Trusting God's *Uncommon* Methods

"Have seven priests carry trumpets of rams' horns in front of the ark. On the seventh day, march around the city seven times, with the priests blowing the trumpets. When you hear them sound a long blast on the trumpets, have the whole army give a loud shout; then the wall of the city will collapse and the army will go up, everyone straight in."

Joshua 6:4–5

✳ Trusting God's *Uncommon* Methods

THE MOMENT OUR NINE-MONTH-OLD DEVELOPED the dexterity to hold our TV remote, she slung it across the room. It slammed to the ground and broke into three pieces. Being a busy, movie-watching family, we quickly fixed the situation by applying duct tape and memorizing a whole new series of movements to get the TV and the remote to connect to each other. This involved a little side-to-side swinging, some serious up-and-down waving, and a whole lot of stretching across the furniture. To anyone looking through our windows, we would have looked crazy.

Some might say that also coming under the umbrella of crazy is the story of the walls of Jericho. What I love about the Bible verses above is the overarching message of trust in the unconventional ways of God.

Jericho was an incredibly well-fortified city, with taller, thicker walls than any of the surrounding cities. And it was directly in the way of the Israelite people as they followed God's instructions and journeyed to their promised land. They took one look at the city with its massive structure and heavy artillery and thought it might be better to just head back to Egypt than to attempt to overthrow it. Yet Joshua remained steadfast, even in the face of great challenges. And God rewarded him rightfully. Joshua was told victory would be theirs if they followed this extraordinary plan: to march around the city once a day for six days and seven times on the seventh day, blowing their trumpets and horns while letting out a huge holler. Can you even begin to imagine the expressions on the Israelite people's faces when Joshua shared that battle strategy? But with God, there's always triumph in the end. Massive walls came tumbling down, and a whole city was destroyed, all because of the Israelites' far-fetched but faith-filled actions.

How inspiring this story can be for you and me. Often, there are unconventional courses and not-so-direct directions set before us in our own careers, educations, seasons of life, and relationships. Left to our own devices, we could eventually wear out from constant swinging, waving, unbalanced stretching, and desperate attempts to get things done our way. But when we act through God's guidance, it's never madness.

He can work through us to knock down walls and show us the next step in our life journey.

Craft: Fabric and Ribbon Tapestry

MATERIALS

Fabric and ribbons in your desired colors
Jute string
Scissors
Tape

INSTRUCTIONS

1. Measure a strand of jute string about four feet long and secure both ends of the string to a table or sturdy surface with tape.

2. Cut the ribbons and fabric into twelve-inch strips.

3. One by one, in your choice of pattern, tie a knot with your ribbons and fabric around the jute. (It will slide, so you can move things around as you work!)

4. Hang and enjoy!

Hope *in* God's Promises

"And we know that in all things God works for the good of those who love him, who have been called according to his purpose."

Romans 8:28

♦Hope *in* God's Promises

IF YOU HAD WALKED INTO MY ROOM when I was a teenager, you could have likely gotten top scores on a quiz about me after spending just a few minutes looking around. You'd have known where I had vacationed, my hobbies, who my favorite people were, and even my life goals and inspirations. How would you have known all this? Because I collected things.

My walls were like a museum showcasing moments in time. I kept ticket stubs, clippings from local newspapers and magazines, mementos from photobooths, tiny notes from relatives and faraway camp friends, awards, and even posters with kittens holding flowers with neon letters spelling "Keep smiling." I held tight to those things because I felt they defined me and illustrated what my life was supposed to be like. I was extremely attached to them, and when a poster ripped or a relationship failed, it felt like a part of me was also broken.

Have you ever felt that way—unhealthily devoted and completely susceptible to what you think should define you? In Romans, Paul reminds his readers that God is always at work—in all things. Not only when you're feeling successful, like when you've won first place, you're dating the perfect guy, or you're sitting front row at your favorite concert, but also during the bad times. Maybe this is the promotion you didn't get, the sting from a harsh text, or the hours of quiet battles fought in your head and heart. Now, let us focus on the best parts of that verse:

> "... God works for the good of those who love him ..."

When you cling to these words instead of fleeting headlines, you can walk boldly in the belief that all you're facing is for your good and His purpose.

Are you feeling tied down? Weary from constantly chasing something that doesn't end up making you feel fulfilled? Slow down and let Him restore you. Try looking around less and looking up more! He's the One who knows you best.

Craft: Rustic Memory Board

MATERIALS

Large empty frame
Jute string
Small clothespins
Hot glue gun or staple gun

INSTRUCTIONS

1. Turn the frame over and unwrap the jute string.

2. Pick a corner of the frame and hot glue or staple the end of the jute string directly to the frame.

3. If you're using hot glue, wait a moment for it to set and cool.

4. Pull the string to a different frame edge, creating a sharp angle, then secure with hot glue or a staple.

5. Continue the pattern, choosing new spots and making sharp angles.

6. Flip the frame over.

7. Allow time for the glue to set and cool before adding anything with your cute clothespins.

Comfort and *God-Given* Riches

"This is what I have observed to be good: that it is appropriate for a person to eat, to drink and to find satisfaction in their toilsome labor under the sun during the few days of life God has given them— for this is their lot."

Ecclesiastes 5:18

❋ Comfort and *God-Given* Riches

I WAS IN THE MIDDLE of a deep clean not long ago when I became instantly overwhelmed by the number of utensils, Tupperware pots, salad bowls, plates, and cups that surrounded me on the floor. There was just not enough storage space to keep them all. Something significant occurred to me through this mundane-but-needs-to-be-done chore. I realized that everything had to be put back in a particular order so that it all could fit. There had to be a proper stacking of plates and bowls, the sliding of long serving dishes on their sides, and my plethora of pots and pans nested from largest to smallest size. And it got me thinking that when things are arranged and weighted correctly, our lives can feel a lot less like a kitchen floor piled high with cookware and more like God created it to be.

In this verse, we are guided to put order, meaning, and a little elbow grease into our daily lives. It's no secret that God has a specific mission for each of us. And surrounding that mission, He also wants to help us keep the important aspects in the forefront and not get lost deep in the lazy Susan. I can easily lose sight of the simple instructions here, pushing priorities further down the list, and be left wondering how everything will possibly fit in the few hours of daylight. We must be diligent in this world to fight the constant temptation to pile up work that doesn't bring us the joy for which we were created. Or, on the flip side, to complain when things get a little crazy. Spoiler alert: they're going to!

Earlier in Ecclesiastes 3:1 are the famous words:

> "There is a time for everything, and a season
> for every activity under the heavens."

So, how can this be applied to our day-to-day lives? Hold fast to these verses, and remember where the balance is between "toilsome" and "labor." It is found when we look to Him for our measure. While there are certainly seasons when we are overwhelmed by the demands we face, there will also be times of calm and restoration. Seek the satisfaction in the work God has ultimately called you to do, and the "good" will follow. And try your best to keep the first things first.

Craft: Painted Bowls and Plates

MATERIALS

Glass plate and/or bowl
Gold acrylic paint
Other acrylic paints in your desired colors
Gold foil paint pen
Gloss finish spray
Small paintbrush and sponge brush
Garbage bag

INSTRUCTIONS

1. Wash your glass plate and/or bowl. Let it dry.

2. Take your glassware outside and place it face down on the garbage bag.

3. Pour a bit of the gold paint into a bowl. Then, dip your smaller brush into the paint bowl and flick the bristles at the glassware with your fingers, splattering the paint in different places over the plate.

4. Repeat until you have a splattered look and a design that you like. Let it dry.

5. Use your gold foil paint pen to paint a small line around the edge of the glassware, still working on the bottom side. Let it dry.

6. With the glassware still on the garbage bag and set face down, pour a small amount of your favorite color paint directly onto the glassware and spread it with a sponge brush. Let it dry.

7. Repeat until it's completely covered.

8. Finally, seal it with the acrylic gloss spray. Let it dry.

9. Hand-wash before and after use.

➤ *Helping* Those in Need

"The King will reply, 'Truly I tell you, whatever you did for one of the least of these brothers and sisters of mine, you did for me.'"

Matthew 25:40

➤ *Helping* Those in Need

IN THE GOSPELS, there are many instances where Jesus departs or reroutes to seek out people in need and He ministers to them right where they are: walking along the road, sitting by a well, or even hanging out in a tree. He was not the type to wait around for someone to come knocking, although that did happen. He was more of a proactive preacher, a forward friend.

Many years ago, I wrote a children's book titled *The Ripple*. It was about a young boy who smiled sweetly at his grumpy doorman. The doorman went on to share his grumpy grin with others in the building, who went on sharing their own smiles with crossing guards, teachers, and kids. Before you knew it, there was a whole community of kindness evolving. I felt compelled to write a story about the power of simple acts of kindness and the difference one individual can make. I often get asked why I wrote the book. My answer?

> Because you never know how your smile and a simple "hello" could change someone's day.

On one amazing occasion, I was on the way to school when I was stopped on the street by a woman. She pulled me aside and said something that still warms my heart to this very day. She told me that every day when we passed each other, I smiled at her. She went on to say that we didn't even know each other, but she was getting ready to move and felt she had to thank me for bringing a little joy to her mornings. We both had tears in our eyes.

Jesus met people and greeted them with the abundance of love, compassion, forgiveness, and direction that they needed at that moment in time. If we look closely around us, we can see souls in need on the street, in the carpool line, waiting at the grocery store, or maybe even pulling water from the water cooler. Ask God for eyes to see and ears to hear, so you can meet people where they are and lead them closer to their Father.

Craft: Farmhouse Check Welcome Sign

MATERIALS

Cutting board
Black chalk paint
Paintbrush
Buffalo check material or ribbon
Scissors
Glue gun
Chalk or chalk pen

INSTRUCTIONS

1. Paint a large square on the surface of the cutting board with the chalk paint.

2. Cut your ribbon or material into four strips. Two of the strips should be cut a little longer than the length of the cutting board, while the other two should be cut a little longer than its width.

3. Fold the material or ribbon in half for a clean line along the edges and hot glue to secure. You should have four folded and glued strips, two short and two long.

4. Glue the strips to the perimeter of the cutting board.

5. Let it dry.

6. Write the message of your choice in chalk and enjoy!

✳ The Strength
of the Holy Spirit

"You, dear children, are from God and have overcome them, because the one who is in you is greater than the one who is in the world."

1 John 4:4

✳ The Strength *of the* Holy Spirit

I LOVE A GOOD JOURNAL. A pretty, flowery, happy-colored, gold-splattered little notebook that will keep my thoughts and feelings tucked safely away. But I concluded a while ago that simply rehashing and overanalyzing what I wrote didn't always result in feeling better. The feelings were expressed, but I didn't have a solid "don't worry about it anymore" game plan afterward. So, I closed the book and continued to worry about it.

The game changer? Talking to God. He already knows everything we're going to write before the pen even hits the paper, and He is ready and willing to send help as we go through the mountains and valleys. This help, this advocate, is the Holy Spirit, and it offers some seriously powerful assistance. In today's verse, John is preparing us for battle—the battle for control over the direction of our hearts and the matter of our minds.

And something big has already happened.

> God has overcome it all by sending His Son to conquer death and darkness through His love.

When you take hold of this truth, the fears, the worries, the insecurities, the lies, the hurting, and all the other tactics the devil uses lose their power over you. He is greater than anything in this world. And you are a child of the great King.

So, when feelings creep up on you and you are overwhelmed, stay the course, look up, open those weary hands, and accept the amazing aid coming directly from Heaven. A small, humble prayer asking for the Holy Spirit to come into your life can turn anything around.

Pray with me, "Come, Holy Spirit." And now begin writing your blessings in your journal. One waiting to be filled with thankfulness, prayers of surrender, and hints of hope. There is no better attack on the devil than looking up for your help and covering yourself in His armor. And never forget that you are marching with an army that has already won.

Craft: Gold Foil–Pressed Prayer Journal

MATERIALS

Writing journal *(any size will do!)*
Gold foil
Metal leaf adhesive
Small sponge brush
Placemat or other protective work surface

INSTRUCTIONS

1. Put your journal on a protective placemat to keep the adhesive and foil from getting on your work area.

2. Using the small sponge brush, spread an even layer of the metal leaf adhesive in the areas of the cover that you want to make shiny and gold.

3. Wait approximately thirty minutes for the adhesive to become clear and very sticky to the touch.

4. Because it can break apart easily, pick up a piece of the gold foil very carefully and transfer it to the journal. The gold foil will only stick to the areas where you spread the adhesive.

5. Using your fingers, gently press down on the gold foil, rubbing the pieces into the paper and covering the sticky areas completely.

6. Wash your hands immediately after the craft is finished. Otherwise, the gold foil will stick with you and glitter everything you touch (which may not be a terrible thing if you like a little sparkle!).

God's *Safety*

"For he will command his angels concerning
you to guard you in all your ways;
they will lift you up in their hands,
so that you will not strike your
foot against a stone."

Psalm 91:11–12

🏺 God's *Safety*

ONE CHRISTMAS, my children and I were decorating the tree. My youngest daughter noticed we didn't have any angel ornaments. I looked all through the boxes scattered across our living room floor and was completely surprised to find that she was correct!

This made me a bit nostalgic, thinking back to the angel perched atop my own childhood Christmas tree. I promised to scour the stores after Christmas and resolve the issue.

The very next day, there was a knock at my door. I opened it to find my darling neighbor, who had become one of my nearest, dearest friends. She simply smiled and handed me an old silver shirt box. I smiled back with a puzzled expression and opened her gift. My heart leaped with joy when I saw what was inside. Angels! It looked like fifty of them, small and large, some made from crochet and others ceramic, one from popsicle sticks, and a handful created from lace. With tears streaming down my cheeks, I asked why she presented me with such a sweet and thoughtful gift. She just replied that she suddenly had a feeling she should give them to me.

The beautiful thing about a Christmas tree covered in angel ornaments is that it serves as a reminder of God's never-ending protection. In Psalm 91, the writer is fully aware of the snares of the devil—the tribulations of the present day. But within this trouble, he is set at ease, knowing that God's loving arms reach further and deeper than any stones the deceiver lays out for him and that His angels will be there to protect him.

What comfort this can provide for us in our daily trials! While there is no promise of pain-free, smooth sailing when we decide to follow our Savior, we can cling to the unshakable truth that we will never walk alone or be without his guidance. Some days, we feel invincible, like nothing can stop us. And other days, we feel tripped up every step we try to take. In all your days, imagine yourself surrounded by a Heavenly army, thwarting threats and dispelling the dark attempts to lead you astray. Rest assured, there is a battle being fought on your behalf every day.

And with such a gift of glorious guardians, what shall we ever fear?

Craft: Sheet Music Angel Ornament

MATERIALS

One sheet of music paper *(bonus if it's from a Christmas song!)*
Thin ribbon in your favorite color
Two-inch wooden gold star
Two-inch wooden bead
Scissors
Glue gun

INSTRUCTIONS

1. Take the piece of sheet music and fold it in half, bringing the top of the paper to meet the bottom. Unfold the paper and cut along the seam, creating two halves. Then, accordion fold each of the paper halves from top to bottom.

2. Take one pleated half for the body, wrap ribbon an inch from the top, and tie it in a bow. Set aside.

3. Take the second pleated half and cut it in half from one long edge to the other. You just created the angel wings!

4. Using the scissors, take your body piece and the two wing pieces and, keeping the pleats closed, cut around the bottom edges of the pleats to make them a curved shape.

5. Take one wing piece and hot glue the tips on one end together, creating a fan. Repeat with the second wing piece.

6. To attach the wings to the body, hot glue the right wing fold to the left side of the body.

7. Now attach the left wing fold to the right side of the body.

8. For the angel head, pull the top of the music paper through the hole in the wooden bead to secure it atop the body.

9. Attach a star as decoration.

10. Bonus: use any remaining string to make a loop so that you can hang your angel on a Christmas tree.

Being Joyful *in* Our Circumstances

"So then, brothers and sisters, stand
firm and hold fast to the teachings we
passed on to you, whether by word
of mouth or by letter."

2 Thessalonians 2:15

✤ Being Joyful *in* Our Circumstances

WHEN COVID-19 FIRST HIT, my sweet parents, who lived states away from their darling grandchildren, wrote each granddaughter their own individual cards. These cards came weekly, each in personalized envelopes, and continued for months and months. What wonderful, heartfelt messages my parents relayed to my daughters by telling stories, asking questions, and sharing updates and much-needed good news and encouragement. And the beauty wasn't only on the inside of the card—it was in the act itself of showing each child how deeply they were loved.

In our verse today, Paul is encouraging his friends and the audience in Thessalonica to continue sharing the good news they have been gifted with. He tells them to "hold fast" to the teachings.

> Paul feared and worried for the faith of those in Thessalonica, and he desperately wanted them to grasp the good news and run with it.

My parents helped my children cling to hope while the news around them said otherwise. Even years later, as we clean rooms and tidy up drawers, I still stumble upon those sweet cards. And they remind me of a time when one believer had the courage to share the gospel of love with anyone who came across his spirit-filled, wonderful words. May Paul be an example to us. What message of encouragement is God calling you to send to someone in your life, near or far?

Craft:
Homemade Cards

MATERIALS

Craft paper
Patterned scrapbook paper
Sticker letters
Twine
Washi tape
Faux paper flowers
Other embellishments and scrapbook pieces of your choice
Pens and colored pencils
Glue
Scissors

INSTRUCTIONS

1. Take your craft paper and fold it in half, then fold it in half again.

2. Open the paper and cut along the middle line, creating two horizontal folding cards.

3. Now you have complete creative freedom! You can use my cards as an example or create amazing cards however you wish.

"Love is patient, love is kind. It does not envy, it does not boast, it is not proud. It does not dishonor others, it is not self-seeking, it is not easily angered, it keeps no record of wrongs. Love does not delight in evil but rejoices with the truth. It always protects, always trusts, always hopes, always perseveres. Love never fails. But where there are prophecies, they will cease; where there are tongues, they will be stilled; where there is knowledge, it will pass away."

1 Corinthians 13:4–8

 *Selfless* Love

THERE IS A REASON many couples choose these verses for their wedding day. Is there any other passage we could read or hear that fully encompasses the beauty, wonder, and complexity of love?

I think back to my own wedding and hearing those words being read out loud. I certainly loved my husband-to-be, but I was gearing up for some serious learning over the next fifteen years! As I grew and experienced this deeper relationship—especially so when I became a parent—I quickly learned that loving someone knocks an ego-centered lifestyle right out of the picture. It was not about me anymore, and boy, did I need help in that new role. Who better to illustrate this than our Heavenly Father when He gave up His one and only blameless Son for our sinful sakes? The ultimate performance of love.

While watching a competition series on TV, I noticed the word "love" was mentioned frequently during the sixty-minute show. After viewing a contestant's act, the judges would speak into the microphone and elaborate on the many reasons why they were so amazing. "I just love you . . ." they'd say at the end. Now, if my standard is not simply the emotion but more the verb, then this scenario doesn't quite match up. Is it possible for a judge to truly love someone after watching them balance forty feet in the air with spoons? I suppose so, but it's not exactly the 1 Corinthians version of love. And that is just the tip of the iceberg.

The amazing, never-failing, prideless, hopeful, joyful word of "love" seems to have lost its meaning in our culture. It's thrown at you by one and all and is more often defined by a fleeting moment of sympathy than by hard-to-come-by perseverance and selflessness.

As St. Augustine is often quoted,
"Love is willing the good of another."

Let us remember the sacrificial love that was poured out for us while we were still sinners. And may this revive our hearts and boost our efforts in the spaces where we find it tough to build bridges.

Notice in today's passage that it does not say that love is perfect. Because we are not, and our love is not. Only God can love us perfectly and model that for us. If we invite God into our imperfections throughout our earthly journey, the possibilities are endless, and so is His love.

Craft: Rope Love Pallet

MATERIALS

Small wooden pallet (*I whitewashed my wooden pallet before starting this craft to help the brown-colored rope pop a bit more.*)
Long strand of craft rope (*two feet long*)
Tacky glue
Paintbrush
Accessories such as paper flowers or artificial flowers

INSTRUCTIONS.

1. Using the tacky glue, spell out the word "love" in cursive across the middle of the pallet.

2. Starting with the top loop of your letter "L," press your rope strand into the glue and continue along 'all the glue letters.

3. Add more glue when necessary and continue to press down to form the word "love."

4. Glue paper or fabric flowers around the pallet. Feel the "love."

✳ A Specific Purpose *for* Us

"For you created my inmost being;
you knit me together in my mother's womb.
I praise you because I am fearfully and
wonderfully made; your works are
wonderful,I know that full well.
My frame was not hidden from you
when I was made in the secret place,
when I was woven together in the depths of
the earth. Your eyes saw my unformed body;
all the days ordained for me were written in
your book before one of them came to be."

Psalm 139:13–16

A Specific Purpose *for* Us

"REFRIGERATOR MATERIAL!" I grew up with that term as a standard for all things worthy of being displayed and admired on our largest and most centrally located kitchen appliance. If it was put on the fridge, it must be important. In my own home, as a mother, I tried to carry on this tradition. However, what once began with praised artwork, stellar report cards, and toothless smiles in school pictures became covered in library overdue notices, tax forms, recipes, and business cards. The important stuff was still there, but it was buried underneath the daily stuff. One might think the fridge wasn't reserved for special pieces anymore.

I remember when one of my daughters asked me where her drawing was. I instantly began to scramble. I knew it was there, but where? I lifted each paper—they were barely kept together under a magnet—as gently as I could. Suddenly, it all came flying off the fridge and covered the floor. My daughter quickly located her rainbow, and she looked at me with big brown eyes that were already tearing up. "Don't you think my picture is beautiful anymore?" I responded with a hug and said, "Of course it is, sweetheart." But she was not convinced, and my heart ached. A week later, we taped up her latest crayon creation together—front and center on the fridge. She approved with a proud and toothless grin.

If I had to picture God's kitchen, it would be like something out of an Ikea magazine, with a fridge door that never runs out of space. All of God's creations would be front and center, proudly displayed for Him to admire and adore. To be "fearfully and wonderfully made" is to be so incredibly unique and individual that there is no one on Earth like you. Not a single person. You are the apple of God's eye. The one who has His heart. He is the proud parent who has you showcased for all the wonderful things you are and will be. And nothing you can do or say will change that. There are days when you might feel like you've been covered up or buried deep under more important things, but God has never forgotten about you.

Close your eyes and imagine your picture on God's refrigerator.

He is so delighted with you. You are His masterpiece.

Rest assured that He wants everyone to know how much He loves you. Start your day by seeing yourself as He does—adored, admired, and worthy.

Craft: Egg Carton Flower Frame

MATERIALS

Frame(s) in your desired size (*I chose a four-by-six inch for this project.*)
Egg cartons (*The number of egg cartons needed may vary—for this project, you'll need 42 egg holders.*)
Scissors
Glue gun

INSTRUCTIONS

1. Cut all the single egg holders from the larger carton(s). You will be using three egg holders, each cut to a different size and nestled inside each other to create a single flower.

2. First, cut a four-petaled flower out of your first single egg holder by cutting four curved petal shapes into the tops of the egg holder.

3. Cut your second egg holder into a medium version of that four-petaled flower by cutting your petals a bit smaller.

4. Now, cut your third egg holder into a smaller version by cutting even smaller petals.

5. Glue the medium flower into the center of the larger flower, rotating it so that the petals do not match up.

6. With the smallest flower, press the petals into each other, creating a "bud." Secure the petals into the bud shape with glue. Glue the bottom of the bud into the center of the medium flower to secure.

7. Repeat steps two through six until you have enough complete flowers.

8. Hot glue the flowers around your frame.

Jesus, *Our* Living Water

"Jesus answered, 'Everyone who drinks this water will be thirsty again, but whoever drinks the water I give them will never thirst. Indeed, the water I give them will become in them a spring of water welling up to eternal life.'"

John 4:13–14

Jesus, *Our* Living Water

"I'VE HAD ENOUGH."

Have you ever uttered those words? Maybe after a long day? During a daunting project? On the losing end of a challenging conversation? I've said those words more than I'd like to admit. We fill up quickly and then spill over. But what are we filling up on?

I'm famous for overcaffeinating and underpraying. I've made time to swing by the Starbucks drive-through, barely making my appointment, but I haven't taken the time to sit and ask God to prepare me for my day, strengthening me through the Holy Spirit. Why am I so quick to tend to my human thirst but not my soul, which is what desperately needs satisfying?

In today's verses, Jesus is tending to the heart of a woman who comes to the well to quench her relentless thirst. But He knows and He sees that she is searching for more. He meets her where she is most vulnerable and reveals exactly where she needs healing and refreshing. We learn her response to this: "Then, leaving her water jar, the woman went back to the town and said to the people, 'Come, see a man who told me everything I ever did'" (John 4:28–29).

This woman can serve as an example for her brave and faithful actions: first, she left her water jar, and second, she told others what she had learned. We cannot walk uphill toward where God wants us to go while still carrying our own heavy jars. That is a beautiful illustration of our faith journey. If we do not try to surrender our hearts and minds, we will continue to be burdened and held back by everything we are holding onto tightly.

As this woman did, may we lay down our jars of what doesn't really fill us.

Let Him be our Living Water, satisfying us the way nothing here on Earth possibly can. And go spread the joyful news of what has changed us! Instead of grumbling, "I've had enough," may we rejoice because He is enough.

Craft: Sharpie Coffee Mug

MATERIALS

White coffee mug *(either regular or travel-sized)*
Alphabet stickers *(bigger sizes if you want to add your initials, smaller sizes if you want to create a word or phrase)*
Permanent markers in a variety of colors

INSTRUCTIONS

1. Decide what you want the mug to say, and place the stickers directly on the mug.

2. Pick out your marker colors.

3. Starting at the edge of the stickers, take your first color and begin to make very close, small dots around the letters, almost as if you are tracing them.

4. Grab your next color and add more dots around the sticker letters, but make these a little further apart.

5. Repeat the pattern with each marker color, lining the stickers and very gradually making the dots more spaced out.

6. Remove the stickers.

7. Bake the mug at 200 degrees Fahrenheit for an hour to set. (Be sure to take off the travel mug top before putting it in the oven.)

8. Hand-wash your mug to keep the design fresh (optional).

Letting Go of Worry

"And why do you worry about clothes? See how the flowers of the field grow. They do not labor or spin. Yet I tell you that not even Solomon in all his splendor was dressed like one of these. If that is how God clothes the grass of the field, which is here today and tomorrow is thrown into the fire, will he not much more clothe you—you of little faith?"

Matthew 6:28–30

Letting Go of Worry

WHEN MY HUSBAND PROPOSED TO ME, I was so incredibly ecstatic that I paid absolutely no attention to the ring he put on my finger that night. It was only in the early morning hours the next day that I woke up with a funny feeling on my left hand and a sparkly diamond reflecting the sunlight. I worked very hard to keep the ring incredibly clean. The new piece of jewelry continued to catch my eye and affection as the weeks and months went by. As I became more accustomed to it on my hand, I continued my daily activities as a kindergarten teacher with all the paint, glue, and dirt you could imagine.

One afternoon, while driving home from school, I realized the ring was no longer as brilliant as it once was. When I arrived home, I scrubbed the ring with soap and water. Much to my dismay, it still wasn't radiant. It was only after a visit to the jeweler that my eyes were opened to what was truly the problem. The sweet man smiled at me when I showed him my hand, and he said, "You can scrub all you want on top, but your beautiful ring can't shine like it's supposed to unless you take it off and get to the bottom of things." And so, I cleaned a little deeper.

We are meant to shine like diamonds, but we need to do a little under-the-surface cleaning sometimes. All our efforts in preserving our outward appearance are in vain. Matthew reminds us that God cares more about us than we could possibly understand, and He wants to be the reason we shine because of the faith deep in our hearts. One look at a flower field, and you can see how much tender care God took when He created such unique and colorful beauty in this world. But we are even more precious than that to our loving Father.

No matter what you have going on along the surface, God can see right through it.

Has your light been covered in dirt and a little darkness? Are there fears and worries deep down that are shadowing you, keeping your true light from shining brightly? Take some time today to hand over those dampening thoughts and leave them at His feet. His freedom can bring you the joy you need to light up this world the way you were meant to do all along.

Craft: Pressed-Flower Lantern

MATERIALS

Mason jar
Pressed flowers
Mod Podge
Sponge brush
Votive candle

INSTRUCTIONS

1. Clean your jar with soap and water. Let it dry.

2. Using the sponge brush, cover the jar with a heavy layer of Mod Podge.

3. Carefully apply your pressed flowers all around the surface of the jar.

4. Reapply the Mod Podge on top of the flowers.

5. Allow it to dry and add your votive candle inside the holder.

God's *Defense*

"Truly he is my rock and my salvation; he is my fortress, I will never be shaken."

Psalm 62:2

➤ God's *Defense*

I USUALLY WALK WITH MY TWO-YEAR-OLD to the playground after elementary school drop-off. It's my morning bribe to get her to comply with so much time spent in the car unloading her three older sisters. My favorite part of our playtime there is when she "hides" in a small plastic house and ducks low, but I can still see her pigtails popping up. She is fully convinced that she is completely out of sight and protected by the faded brick walls and broken swinging door around her. After counting loudly to ten, I tiptoe over and happily announce that I've found her. She looks at me with a combination of shock and joy, quickly requesting we do it all over again.

Walking back to the car one day, I realized she is not all that different from me at times. We both seem to have taken a false sense of security in our surroundings. My home, job, friendships, and even my health—all those things are built on shifting sand. They are simply not strong enough to withstand all our hardships on their own.

By stark contrast, today's verse from Psalms paints the beautiful picture of God being our rock, a fortress. What amazing imagery of solid ground underneath us and encompassing us! These words meant so much to the Psalmist, David, that he repeated them verbatim four verses later, along with comforting text such as "rest" and "hope." When something is repeated in the Bible, it is a caution light with a bright arrow directing us to pay attention.

Surely, we will have times when our focus and attention are on the things shifting around us. It is our fallen human nature to seek shelter within plastic walls and behind broken doors. How will we know these things won't guarantee our security?

We can ask a question: "When I hide behind _____ , how safe do I feel?"

Because none of these are meant to last, we might find ourselves answering, "Not that safe at all." But a fortress is meant to protect and guard through the most crippling of invasions.

I encourage you to run to God when you need protection. Resist the urge to fight on your own or build up walls that will only crumble when the enemy throws his attacks. Your Father longs to be your refuge, so rest in the arms of the One who seeks you out and joyfully announces, "You are found."

Craft: Painted Rock Art Holders

MATERIALS

River rocks
Paint pens
Gold wire
Artwork of choice

INSTRUCTIONS

1. Wash the river rocks and let them dry.

2. Decide on your designs and paint them directly onto the top of your rocks.

3. Unwind approximately two feet of your gold wire and cut it.

4. With one end, wrap the wire around the middle part of the first rock five or six times, ending at the top.

5. On the underside of the rock, wrap the loose end of the wire perpendicularly under and around the center bunch of wires five or six times and pull tightly after each wrap to hold them together.

6. From the center of the painted side of the rock, create a stem with the wire. At the top of the stem, circle the wire around your finger tightly a few times to make the artwork holder.

7. Add your artwork and enjoy!

✳ God, *the* Ultimate Maker

"But now, O LORD, you are our Father;
we are the clay, and you are our potter;
we are all the work of your hand."

Isaiah 64:8
(ESV)

✳ God, *the* Ultimate Maker

IN ONE OF MY FAVORITE MOVIES, *The Greatest Showman*, the song "A Million Dreams" sounds exactly like a conversation between God and myself. Every time I hear my children singing along to it, I smile. I truly think I am talking to God about the things keeping me up at night, swimming in my head—such as words, ideas, projects, and how I really want to use them to make the world a better place. And He listens. And He responds. And I know He is wanting and asking to be a part of it all— for me to share my dreams and bring Him along.

As I worked on creating this book, some of the crafting projects went perfectly and as planned. Others required me to walk away, revisit, and reinvent. And some even got completely tossed because they just didn't work. From materials to methods, each creative endeavor served as an opportunity to adapt, trust, surrender, and open my hands just a little bit more. Most importantly, each moment of this journey was a chance to bring along my Heavenly Father, my Maker. I found myself trusting in Him more.

> I knew He was there, watching over me, guiding me and leading me in everything I built.

When I think about the beautiful relationship between the clay and the potter, like in today's verse from Isaiah, it reminds me of "A Million Dreams." But this time, God is the creative mind behind it all, the One brimming over with visions and a million dreams for us.

We are that clay. And unless we are shaped, molded, and worked, we remain a lump of clay and never truly know or become what we could be. Inviting Him into our lives frees us to be plucked from our former foundation, lifted to a whole new level, with Living Water added to us, and ultimately put on the potter's wheel to be turned into something we were uniquely destined and designed for. The process can be difficult, with bends and twists we never requested. There may even be the fire of unwanted stress and pressure we feel coming from all sides. But if we rely on Him—who is greater than our own strength—to make it through, what might be the result?

Is it time you trusted in your Potter, the One who takes time to mold you, hold you, and stay with you as you chase a million dreams breathed into you? In the end, He will reveal to you what so few could even begin to see— something stronger, complete, and wonderfully made. What might happen if you cooperated in God's creative process and worked hand-in-hand with the Creator of the universe? Oh, dear friend, I am on the edge of my seat, waiting to find out.

Craft: Wire Word Art

MATERIALS

Printed-out cursive word
Wire *(Twenty-gauge is best, but I used what I had from previous crafts.)*
Clear tape
Scissors

INSTRUCTIONS

1. Lay your printed word flat on a table.

2. Begin with one end of your wire and trace the first letter of your cursive word.

3. Tape the wire down after you mold each letter.

4. After you finish the whole word, remove the pieces of tape.

5. Add your wire word to a plant by securing two pieces of cut wire to the first and last letters, or simply display it on the wall.

Acknowledgments

To my husband, who steadily fed me coffee as I wrote in the early hours of the morning and watched and bathed the babies as I continued typing through dinner and into the hours of the night. Thank you for your never-ending support of my writing dreams. And for letting me make things. Lots and lots of things. I love you.

To my beautiful band of daughters, who are always boosting my creative juices and supplying me with stories upon stories. And who happily helped me craft away for the examples in this book. I pray these pages inspire you to create with your Maker and bring you closer to Him.

To my parents, for constant and prayerful support in chasing dreams rooted in God's gifts. I cannot wait to sit on the couch and read these pages with you both by my side. Thank you for inspiring me through your love and wisdom.

To my wonderful brother and sister, who never cease to cheer me on in every adventure.

To my friend Becky, who scoured and searched and prayed as she help me put this concept together from the moment she first heard the idea. It wouldn't be a book without you! I am forever grateful. And for all the photography fun we had!

To my fabulous friends, Kerri and Mariana, who drop everything to dance the happy aisles of Hobby Lobby with me, showing up with loads of laughter and warm hugs.

To my Walking with Purpose warriors and those at St. Mary's, for preparing me with Bible verses and bringing a passion for God's love story into my daily life. And for praying through this exciting journey!

To my amazing editors Olivia and Lindsay, for believing in this manuscript from the very beginning. I am beyond blessed by your guidance and vision. Thank you for bringing this project from a simple dream to real life!

To the whole Paige Tate & Co. team, for putting together a book more beautiful than I could ever imagine.